GORILLA

LIFE CYCLES

Words that look like **this** can be found in the glossary on page 24.

BookLife
PUBLISHING

©2018
BookLife Publishing
King's Lynn
Norfolk PE30 4LS

All rights reserved.
Printed in Malaysia.

A catalogue record for this book is available from the British Library.

ISBN: 978-1-78637-382-3

Written by:
Holly Duhig

Edited by:
Madeline Tyler

Designed by:
Danielle Rippengill

CONTENTS

WHAT IS A LIFE CYCLE?

All animals, plants and humans go through different stages of their life as they grow and change. This is called a life cycle.

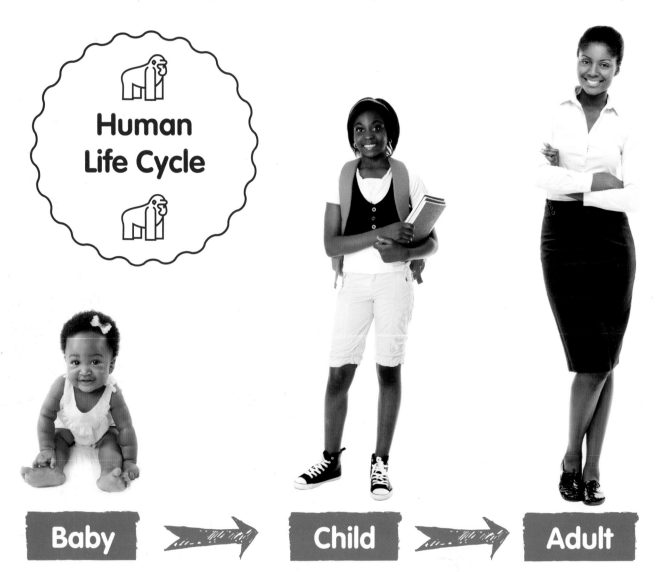

Human Life Cycle

Baby ➡ Child ➡ Adult

WHAT IS A GORILLA?

Gorillas are a type of ape. They are **mammals** that live in groups called troops usually led by one male gorilla, called a silverback.

Silverback

INFANTS

Baby gorillas are called infants. Female gorillas are usually **pregnant** for eight and a half months and tend to give birth to one infant at a time.

Infants drink their mother's milk to grow big and strong.

Gorillas usually weigh around 1.8 kilograms when they are born.

Their hands and feet have a very powerful grip which means they can cling onto their mother's fur.

As gorilla infants get older, they grow and change. When they are about nine weeks old, infants begin to crawl and explore the world around them.

However, infants still stay close to their mothers for protection. Once they are strong enough, they climb onto their mother and ride around on her back.

Gorilla infants are carried by their mothers until they are four years old.

GROWING GORILLAS

Gorillas build nests out of plants to sleep in at night. Infants sleep in their mother's nest for the first two to three years of their lives.

A female gorilla in her nest.

When infants are older, they begin to eat food such as fruit, plant stems and sometimes **termites**. They also learn to build their own nests.

GORILLAS

Female gorillas become adults when they are ten years old. Female gorillas will often leave the troop they were born in to find a **mate** and have **offspring** of their own.

A Troop of Gorillas

Male gorillas are bigger than female gorillas.

Adult males start to grow silver hair on their backs, which is why they are called silverbacks. They also leave their troop to find a mate.

DIFFERENT GORILLA SPECIES

Mountain gorillas live on the Virunga Mountains in Africa.

There are two **species** of gorilla: the eastern gorilla and the western gorilla. Mountain gorillas are a type of eastern gorilla.

Cross River gorillas live in Nigeria and Cameroon, in Africa.
They have slightly reddish fur and are **endangered.**
There are only 300 in the wild.

Cross River gorillas are a type of western gorilla.

GORILLAS IN THE WILD

Just like humans, gorillas stick to a daily routine. They eat in the mornings and evenings and play, sleep or groom one another in the middle of the day.

These mountain gorillas are wrestling.

Gorillas usually live between 35 to 40 years in the wild. When gorillas become old, the younger members of the troop look after them.

GLORIOUS GORILLAS!

Gorillas are very clever. They can even be taught **sign language**. Koko, a gorilla born in the USA, has been taught over 1,000 words in sign language!

Gorillas hardly ever need to drink water. They get enough water to survive from the plants that they eat.

WORLD RECORD BREAKERS

Oldest Gorilla

The world record for the oldest known gorilla goes to Colo. Colo was born in **captivity** and was 60 years old when she died.

On the 31st of October, 2009, the world record for the largest gathering of people dressed as gorillas was made! The event raised money for mountain gorilla **conservation**.

LIFE CYCLE OF A GORILLA

1 A female gorilla gives birth to an infant.

2 The infant learns to crawl and climb onto its mother.

LIFE CYCLES

3 The infant becomes an adult and leaves the troop to find a mate.

4 The gorilla is ready to have offspring of its own.

GET EXPLORING!

Gorillas are an endangered species, so they are often kept in conservation centres to keep them safe. Why not see if you can go and visit one?

GLOSSARY

captivity kept in a zoo or safari park and not in the wild

conservation work that is done to protect something from damage or harm

endangered when a species of animal is in danger of becoming extinct

mammals an animal that has warm blood, a backbone and produces milk

mate a partner (of the same species) who an animal chooses to produce young with

offspring the child or young of a living thing

pregnant when a mother develops a baby inside of her

sign language a way of communicating using hand gestures and signs, used by people who are deaf

species a group of very similar animals or plants that are capable of producing young together

termites pale, soft-bodied insects that live in colonies usually in hot countries

INDEX